III

JONATHAN LOVEJOY

ELIZABETHAN

The Complete Poems of Elizabeth Peele

Volume III

Armageddon Publishing

Cover: *Aurora,* 1881
William Adolphe Bouguereau (1825-1905)

ISBN-10: 0692319182
ISBN-13: 978-0692319185

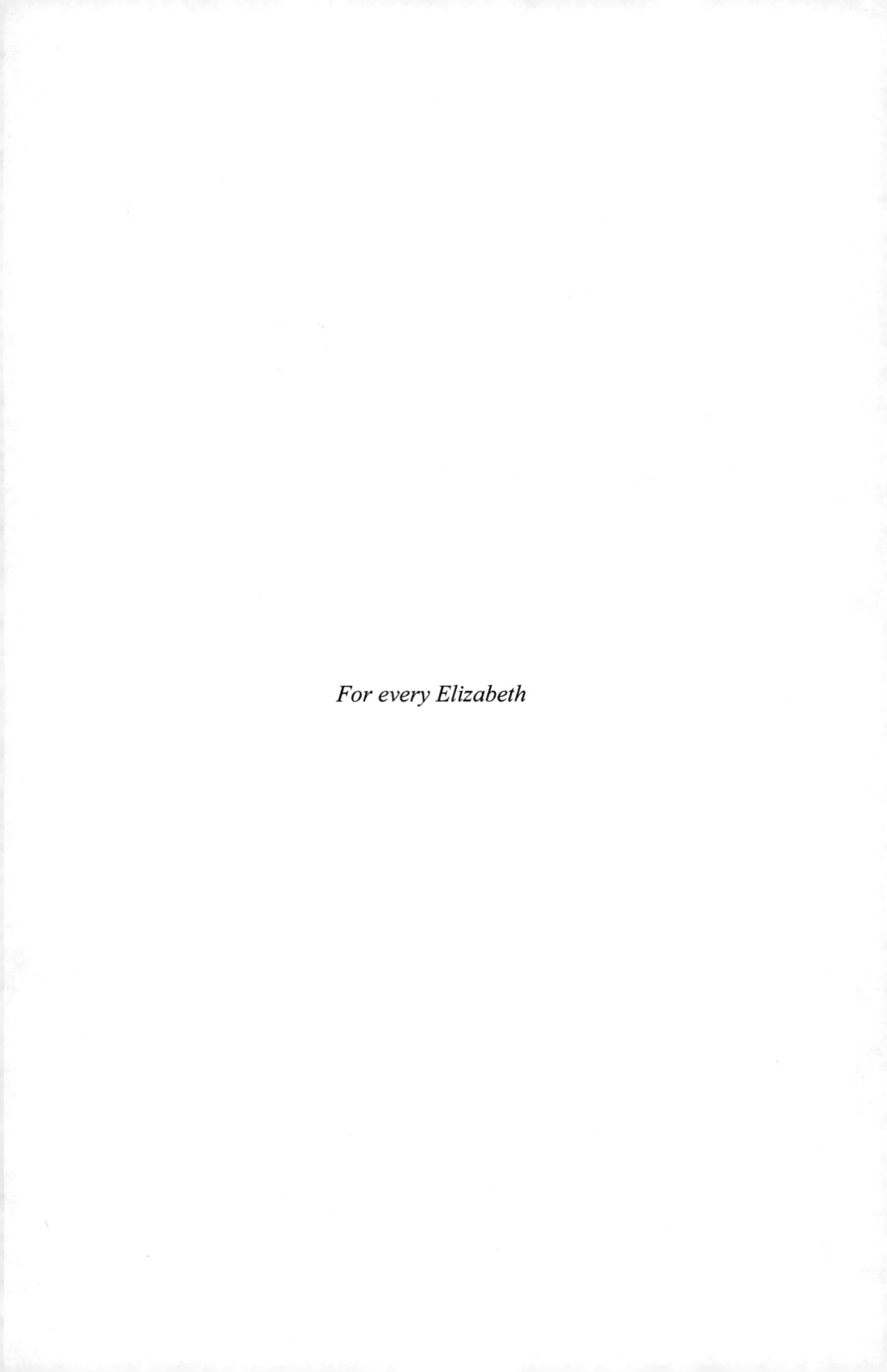

For every Elizabeth

Introduction

Carmen Angelina Coletti (Elizabeth Peele) was perhaps the greatest composer who ever lived. After her death, studies of her music revealed a body of work—almost exclusively instrumental—of such beauty and power as to defy description. Even so, her lifelong reclusiveness rendered them obsolete to the world, and these musical treasures may remain apart from public view forever.

Even those few who heard her original scores did so in quiet apprehension, that this beautiful widow—lost somewhere deep in North Carolina farming country—brought forth music as completely ingenious as any ever written before. The sounds of greatness flowing from this woman's piano, surely this is not meant to be! For what purpose can she truly serve as a neoclassical composer in a jaded modern world, except as a curiosity and eventually, a fountain of eternal exploitation?

But while music did serve as a profession for her since she was twelve—her only wage being a sound mind and spirit—there was still another expression, both private and unintentional, equally meant for her eyes only. Gathered posthumously, so few of these "assemblies" can be called unique or special, and likely cannot set her apart from any other lonely poet in the world. But still they live on, as a glimpse into the mind of a musical genius and abused woman of Faith. Written parallel to her music over the years—with no striving for greatness or immortality—these poetic trifles, ironically, may be the only compositions of hers the world will ever hear.

or

"The Assemblies"

Volume III

Such is the grandest music among us—

Poets…

Such are the wildest thoughts among us—

Composers…

The Book of Mary

60th Assembly

303

LITTLE GIRLS have powers

As this has always been true

So shall it ever be

Running…

Playing, Jumping

Laughing, Living

Crying…

Dying in the rain

Yelling pain from homelives of shame

Marks of pain from mothers

Whatever happened to Janey Reardon?

They took her body away

When her mother beat her to death—

Janey Reardon was buried today—

In the rain

304

DEVASTATION booms from skies of fury
Cracking
Splitting Creation in two
Rumbling the earth from sea to shore

Speaking the voice of doom
Of judgment
Of Redemption
Of Salvation

305

The umpdillyicious trail
The scrumptillyicious mail
Waiting to be born

It confounds the reason of man
Making him think that everything is fine
When it most certainly is not!

EVERWOOD forever would be burning

Charred in ashes and soot

A crime is afoot here!

Where the aardvark kneels to play…

To pray

61st Assembly

IS SHE a lesbian?

She doesn't know

All of her life she has wondered

Attracted to girls…

Attracted to women

Loving men but hating them just the same

Wishing to be free from these constraints

These restraints

The restrictions of marriage

Where a permanent friction rules

A churning

A yearning…

Burning beneath cultured civility

SHE sits in church with the rest of them
Waiting…
Awaiting the fluff to take substance
To have purpose and meaning

It's hot in this Hell of waiting
Skating across thin ice
Where feeble brains stay the course of Hiptology
Wherefore doth thou lay thy logic

Thy reason?

Church is a refuge
A home for Spirit thought
For spirit walking
For talk of Spirits

It is where they come through single file
Walking from their lives to gather
Stalking the edge of lies to wander
To wonder if there really is a healing force

A place where all of this will end someday
Beyond the grave

Morning is a special time
A special place
When the body is most receptive to ideas
Moving to its own pace in the grand scheme

Lifting dreams from the night shade
From the brigade of the night before
Morning is a place where pain flows the most free
The most unabated

The most undisturbed

310

THE VIOLIN is a witness to this
It sings a poignant melody in the breeze
It conspires with the other strings
Left on its own to sing when the bars have passed

Listening to the winds come together
To breathe Heaven's Melody upon the earth
When the violin sings a melody
It knows…

It grows…
It flows Beauty into the world

311

Shed a new light on this space in time
On this old situation
It is not your time to die
Nor your desire to writhe in poverty

Ingenuity speaks
To whisper your path down a new trail
To show you the way to a new life
A life away from pain

A time apart from poverty
To live…

To prosper

62nd Assembly

312

IN the Land of the Dead
Spirits ride the wind
Without facts
Grieving their birth

Without hope
Seeking obliteration
Annihilation
Release from suffering

313

Evil moves across the floor
Gliding through the walls
Peeking behind closed doors
Hiding in the mirror

Seeking

314

WHEN THE SEED of harvest is sown
There is nothing to do but wait
Wait for the reaping
The reward

315

A SUDDEN heavy rainfall
Raindrops pelting the earth
Jumping, splashing
Dancing, prancing all about

Each drop having its own purpose
Its own destiny
Seeking its own way to go

The rain falls from high in the sky
Splashing the ground below
Replenishing…
Renewing life

316

THUNDER rolls gently after the rain

The sound of apocalypse

Calling from the future…

Echoing

317

THE SOUND of blessing comes from the clouds
after the stormy wind has passed
the voice of heaven cries a reward
across the blighted plain

from a great distance the voices ring
for time
for history
for life

63rd Assembly

318

Little Robin Redbreast
Hopped across the lawn
Searching for a worm to eat
Before the break of dawn

Little Robin Redbreast
Flew high into a tree
To sing a happy morning song
A lovely melody

319

Ghosts threaten to appear
In the halls of perpetuity
In the halls of poverty
Where desperation waits

Inspiration burns a hole in space
Revealing ingenuity
The path to life
To prosperity

320

SHE is the flower, the beautiful—
The living Death

The pain of eons lives in her eyes
It colours every corner
Every contour of her paleness
Every edge of her darkened spirit

The curls of her midnight hair
Are born from Infinity's Sorrow
Exhaustion…gloominess…grief…
Weariness and melancholy bear up her weakness

Her strength is the power of love
Her agony, her anguish
Her power is what she knows
What she loves…

She knows the grave
She loves the eternal sleep

321

She said, "If you're bothered by it"
"Feed it to the Lions!"
They know the way
They know the hour of its passing

You still can't compete with Spirits
Every universal purpose is given to them
They know every reason under the Sun for why you fail
For why you cannot pay the Piper's Main...

She said, "If you're still bothered by it"
"Feed it to the Lions!"
Abstain from wickedness—
Morality will see you through!

322

It pours from the fountain of life
Roaring forth like a Lion Beast
Feasting on souls
Tearing men asunder

Springs reek
From Thundering skies of Apocalypse
Rain pours down on Maynor's Day
On the way of mountains

Peaches, plums, apple blumgarden
Pears, witches and the fruit of sin
Forbidden to those in flesh and blood
Hidden from those in the Mud of Life

Stop feeding damnation to your soul!
You shall not escape it!

323

Appleplumb cake baking in the oven
Showing her the way to go
It is the way of things
The way her life is supposed to be

Kitchens and every other room
Are filled with the laughter of children
It is the false laughter of dying hope
Put there by demons

Made into sadness
Futures born and raised in poverty

324

How do we get up and out of this young adulthood?

Pain rains down…

Like a splash of red

A flash of dread and blood

64th Assembly

325

Say goodbye moon!
Your days of turning are over!
No more weeping—
No more howling over affairs of men

Now you will perish in a burning
A blazing fire of cosmic indifference
Your light will go out in a blaze of glory
In a haze of fire and blood

Leap from the sky, Moon!
Fall to Earth and die!

In the soil of life and living
Truth grows
Sprouting leaves
Blossoming

In the soil of life and living
Lies grow
Choking the truth—
Killing it

Jumping around with the trumpet
Whirling, twirling
Thumping ears with the piccolo
The bassoon laughs at your inadequacy…

The cello mourns for it

Don't cry for the viola!
It does not envy the violin
They master their own course in life
Their own merry way!

Mournful clarinets, biting oboes
Soulful basses
All have purpose
They are the sound of what is predestined

Playing by another's will and desire
Blessed with beauty
Cursed with ugliness
Helpless along the way

What world is this?

Where people carry guns
To shoot each other
Where people carry knives
To stab each other with

Where security and precaution must be taken
To protect people from one another?

65th Assembly

The sound of war thunders overhead
The sound of killing
Of dying

Whirling blades…
Lifting souls to their final day
Flying them to their death

Their Honor

330

Somewhere in the Land of Dreams
Beyond the next horizon
There is a forest that grows
A Blue Forest

Rows of trees packed tightly together
With tall, healthy trunks of white wood
White branches spreading out…
Into a Crown of Beauty

Around these branches grow leaves
As to defy description
Leaves of midnight blue
Rippling ever so slightly in the breeze

And somewhere in this field of blue
Is a single spot of crimson
One bright red leaf to see
To contrast with the field of midnight

And the wood of Crimson White

Among the trees, upon a new Earth
Somewhere beyond the sea
There is a place where the power of Love can be found
A place where the Blue Forest grows

Among the trees of melancholy beauty
Is the single red leaf to see

331

Three curtains of silk
Flowing gracefully to the floor
Folding in upon themselves
Each bearing a color of the Trinity

One is the color of nature
The green of Creation
The other is the color of blood
The red of Redemption

The final curtain is between the other two…

Or even to the left of them
Or even to the right
This is the color of the sun
The glowing color of pale moonlight

The color of Salvation

These are unfurled during the winter season
The season of lost hope and shattered dreams
Colors of Life
Love…

And Laughter

332

I asked them to help me
In the days before prosperity
Underneath the cloak of poverty
In the accursed land of rain

I learned that they were liars
Underneath voices of civility
Lies spoken as outright truth
Politeness to an extreme

They had no desire for my success
Refusing to help me
Now they must endure the pain
The agony

The anguish of knowing that my success still came
Even though they refused to help me
They have learned to master sincerity
To lie with the voice of truth

So that they can never be rightly accused
Of the pain they have inflicted

333

Three angels from another place
Appeared in time of greatest need
Bringing comfort to a broken vessel
Soothing relief upon a weary soul

334

ALL OF US are guilty
But it still begs the question
Why are we so cruel…
To one another?

66th Assembly

335

A wife burned in the fire of lust
To a man she was never married to
Consequences were made clear in the stars
Results of what she had to do

She bore a heavy mark of Sin
As her lover beamed his foolish pride
Her betrayal incurred the Wrath of Ages…
A shattered marriage for the adulterous bride

A drama plays out in the stars
The story of man and woman
A tale told time and time again
For all the world to see

Erlina! Pamina!
Where have you gone?
Come back to your husband's love!
To your husband's loving arms!

A drama plays out in the stars…
The story of infidelity

337

I feel trapped
Trapped by my own body
Trapped by my own birth
Trapped by God himself

I have nothing to do
I have nowhere to go…

Incogneto is the way of the new laureate
They hide underneath social skills
Underneath the invisible cloak
A cloak of morality that hides their true intentions

They never mention the pain they cause
Nor the pain they are in
They are drained of the Stuff of Gods
The Reign of Kings is dead

Things like this happen because, apparently…

You're not ready
You're not prepared for what awaits you
The fate you have is coming

But don't hate it

Rather wait for its arrival
You may not be given to survival
But this is the way of things
The order of existence

67th Assembly

340

What city is she from?
To what city is she going?
Is it snowing where she lives?
Does she endeavor to break through?

341

Gillian and Lillian
Are both too silly for me
Both girls have lost their way to the party
Their drinking days are over

Twin girls have left this world
In a blaze of fire
And now their parents have to mourn
When they are buried

342

When it comes down to it
You are wasting your time
What good is there in life?
Except for blessed sleep

Sleep carries the soul aloft
Above the swamp of human corruption
High above the Earth
To a place where dreams live and grow

Where goodness has power

343

The crowd laughs on
Smiling genuine disinterest
Real discontent
Smiling their lack of concern

This happens…
While the helpless woman is carried away
In shrieks and screaming
Somewhere from within

It never pays to be jaded to Dymler's Crossing
The path which paved the way to this present
To this future

O Dear!
He tried to capture her attention with a Harp!
Now he has her bound in ropes
Ropes of wicked intent

68th Assembly

344

He sat alone in his room

Brooding

"I'll hang them", he said

And then he was dead

Pain pours from clouds of fury
While the train speeds from over the horizon
Chords of manic ingenuity play
While sorrow slams on Melancholy's Door

Queen Lear looks on from the grave
Grieving for the entire Earth
The chorus sings destruction down upon the Land
Melodies of flood and doom

346

Say goodbye Paula", was the word

As she lay underneath the Power of Blood

They pulled a gun near her head…

I want a new life

A new place to go

I am weary of exile

Tired of the sound of silence

The sound of nothing

The feel of the air around me

I desire another place to see

New faces

New voices

A new way to spend my days

I want to go outside…

And feel the breeze upon my face

I desire to leave my prison behind forever

To go the Land of Freedom

The Spirits are rebuked
In the name of our Lord
They have no power over humanity
Except for what little is given

They operate because of the Curse of Eden
The curse of Adam and Eve
But someday the burden of sin will lift
And their power will be shaken…

Taken

Listen to the music of the world
Melodies in the air around you
Whispering from the trees
In the song of the whistling bird

Even in the creak of every old house
In the click of every switch
All is borne from predestiny
All are signs to hearken

They foretell the future
They solve mysteries from the past
Every answer is in the sound of life
In the music of the world around us

350

I desire to see the sky
To see the clouds of heaven
But I am buried beneath the ground
In a grave

Release me from my tomb!
Let me see life with living eyes!

69th Assembly

351

Two little spirits
Came drifting toward me
Two little girls
Spirits of innocence grown

Maria Marianna…
A face of Beauty
Confidence bestowed
A future of happiness and friendships galore

Carmelita Angelina…
Whom they call Carmen
A little face burdened with uncertainty
A fearfulness of the world around her

Two roses in bloom
White Roses

Replete with power
The glory of Purity
Innocence…
And Spiritual Love

352

She woke up in a land of plenty
A woman with nowhere left to go
People were prosperous to infinity
With no more charity left to show

An angel from the Wealthen Stream
Said *"you can't stay here any more"*
So she gathered the blankets of her darkest dream
And took her poverty out the door

353

At the end of the Grand Competition
Waiting for barriers to fall
They hoped to end the family tradition
Of having no success at all

354

He gazed upon a fine reflection
Strength and vitality
A promise of a healthy future…
A life of prosperity

From the mist of a troubled sleep
Arose a ghostly garble
A warbling voice of lost hope
A feeble attempt at living

The voice of the living dead
Not knowing that death is better
Skipping through life unawares
Heading towards the grave

356

Whistling messages from the trees
Warnings disguised in song
"The word of the day is cataclysm!..."
Coming upon the Earth

The birds have known it from the beginning…
The end of the age is near
This part of history is winding down
To where Time will cease to be

70th Assembly

357

Speeding towards the Land of the Dead
Red and yellow, KILL -a- fellow
Looking to do one final sin
Then laying down to die

358

Along a dark and perilous road
On her journey towards the Land of Freedom
She wears the color of a sunny sky
With a heart that burns a fire of virtue

Lost along the dark and perilous road
Her face is touched by Crimson
A tickling
A prickling

From her nose a trickling of blood…

I am haunted by death
The spirit of it
Taunting me
Making me afraid to sleep

Haunting

The race is not given to the swift
Nor the strong
But he that endures until the end
Will be victorious

Run until the race is done
Until you reach your goals
Run your pace to the setting sun
Until the race is—

361

She woke up from her sleeping bed
With no knowledge of what she had to do
She went to find the Blackness Man
To learn what it is she had to do

You have died today
Although you wanted to live
Your body has passed away
Because it had no more life to give

You wander though the Land of the Living
Though you belong to the Land of the Dead
What was the point of years of giving
To die alone in your sleeping bed?

71st Assembly

Little girls are a glimpse of Heaven
A light of innocence
Of beauty
And Purity

They are the beginning of life
The creation of it
Seeking to learn the Path to Virtue
The Road to Heaven

364

It is DESTINY…

It cannot be stopped
It cannot be made to go
It moves under its own power
It is living…

Breathing…

Never pull a truth from the Dobbin Tree
It is truth laced with lies
A bitter fruit of lying poison
A poisonous twist of bitter deceit

Those that tell this truth are liars indeed
Bearing false witness against their neighbor
Hiding what they know
Concealing the truth in a lying tongue

They pulled this fruit from the Dobbin Tree
A place where evil communications grow
Where the seed of untruth was planted
Blossoming from a soil of immorality

Speak no truth from the Tree of Lies
It is truth laced with deceit
Fruit as bitter as wormwood
As poisonous as bile

Treasure the Passage of Time

The removal of each new day

The renewal of hope

The tomorrow

Fear and Pain are all that I have known

And now, Death shall accompany them

This is the end of rain…

The beginning of days of heaven

There must be a time to rest
A time to dream no more
To recover from the burden of hoping…
The agony of longing

Life is charged with the energy of broken dreams
The pain they cause is power
Strength for the journey
On the road to the Land of Freedom

72nd Assembly

He grabbed the rattlesnake by the tail
To drag it out of the house
It bit his thumb above the nail
Killing the abusive louse!

370

If they reject you 90 times
Do you bother to try again?
They said, *we don't want your stories and rhymes*
Ninety multiplied by ten!

Two times they said, you were the best
Little stories too weak and thin
Nine hundred times you failed the test—
Why bother to try again?

371

Ghosts fade in from horror's way
Teaching their sorrow to a rainy day
While the road to freedom is in Melancholy Bay
Flooding every hour of tomorrow away

372

Somewhere in the grieving land
Beyond the rising sun
In the Valley of Despair
Where hope has gone to die

Amazing cisterns play
Underneath clouds of melancholy gray
Where the pain of expectation ends—
Where hope fades away

373

Avarice squeezes by on Beauty
Looking like a Loft Maiden
Old layers are shattered like glass
Killing the one who falls against it

Fear does no good
When the demon has come to get you
There is nowhere left to run
Nowhere to hide

73rd Assembly

374

Sons of the men of earth
Hearken to the Voice of Man
I have seen the manner of my death
The way of my passing

As I burn the red and blue flame
Yellow shall extinguish it
Dignitaries shall not attend my funeral
Nor shall those I have not liked

I have writhed in poverty for a lifetime
Now I writhe in the torment of death

375

SATAN could terrify us beyond description
There are tricks at his disposal
Evil that would show us the truth
Causing our hearts to fail

But the Spirit of God holds him at bay
Not letting him show us the Meaning of Fear
Making his presence feeble
Weak by comparison to what it could be

376

Speeding the abomination trail
A prisoner of mankind's evil way
In fear of a world under the Devil's Veil
Grieving for the warming Light of Day

Gaze at the plight of the flightless man
The homeless man
You've been talking about helping him for years…
Haven't you?

Maybe someday, you'll get around to compassion
To charity
The homeless man is a blight
A blight on what we hold dear

One droggy day, you decide to help him
But where is he?
The homeless man has gone away…
To his Homeland

Thy face shines in the cloud
The face of eternity
Flowing…
A glowing mountain of righteousness

The glory of Heaven is revealed in the cloud
Billowing purity into the sky
Shimmering brilliance
Glimmering Hope and Faith for this age

For this eternity

379

Beauty touched the woman of virtue
Of a kind only known to a blessed few
Happiness appeared to have graced her true
When joy smiled brightly as her loveliness grew

74th Assembly

380

She came to me under cloak of night
A sign I welcomed with a nod
I saw her name in blocks of Light
And then I felt the power of God

Melodies brighten my darkest day
To soothe my aching sorrow away
Harmonies call from beyond the sea
Inspired golden ingenuity

A songbird flies the distant land
Above the shores of Azurean Sand
Now a memory brightens my darkest day
To soothe my aching sorrow away

Voices sing from across the sea
On golden strings of melody
A songbird hath flown to infinity
To bring beauty to the shores of eternity

Now a songbird lives in Days of Lore
Calling from a peaceful shore
Sending melodies to rule my darkest day—
To soothe my aching sorrow away

Be wary of dreams
Demons will appear as Angels
Expounding wisdom
Speaking lies

But a dream from God is Truth…
Revealing the path of life

383

Speeding through the Land of the Dead
As if there was a place to go
Daylight turns upon thy darkest dread
Showing demons from the ground below

384

They laughed to ease away the pain
Asian beauties in a dining stand
Natural blondes came in from the pouring rain
The reasons they light'ned every dark'ned strand

75th Assembly

Coins…

What pretty things!

Small

Precious

Inspiring life…

And death

386

Gods play games in the rolling blue
Leaping from one side of heaven to the other
Gods appear as clouds in the sky
Bringing beauty to our warmest day

Bringing melancholy above Winter's Crying
Sounding power across the roaring waves
Soaring high into the sky above
Flying upon whims of eternity

Mountains of beauty
A sea of devastation

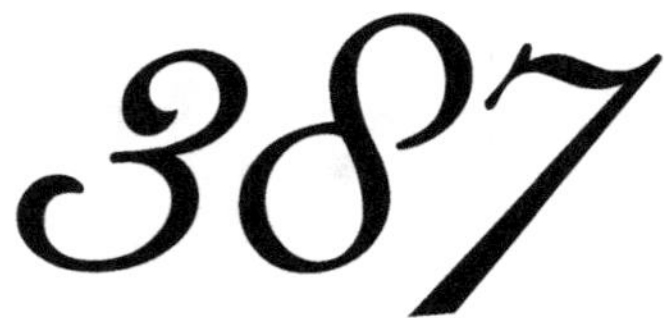

He traded away the blue chariot
For a red one he didn't need
Then regret roped him like a lariot
The consequences of his greed

He traded away the blue rooster
For a red one he didn't need

When you go around the Red Corner
You believe you have found the way up
But the Red Corner is the way down
The path to devastation

Go around the Blue Corner instead
It is sufficient for what you need

76th Assembly

Prevent children from self indulgence

Over indulgence

They will run with the Wind and the Tide

Until they have drowned

Tell them what to do

And what not to do

Provide them with guidance

A center of morality

Demons lie in wait for them

Lurking

Seeking them out

Hoping to corrupt their minds and bodies

Their souls

390

The Earth itself may be under a curse

People should all beware

Because of the harm that must be done…

Because of the evil

391

For the accursed, for every living thing
There is shared a common gift
A focal point of strength
In the midst of prolonged suffering…

It is the knowledge that Time will pass
And that all things must pass away

392

In a persons's life, there are points of clarity
Moments that enlighten the senses
Until there is perception of a Greater Force
A Higher Power

Infusing the mind with revelation--
That life is perhaps nothing more
Than a flowering of what is foreordained
The fulfillment of a Divine purpose

Destiny and Fate…
Through the Will of God.

77th Assembly

393

High above the Coral Sea
Rises two towers of earthen beauty
One as white as mountain snow
The other as blue as the sea below

On the edge of the Marble Wasteland
Is a shore of ivory sand
From there, the two towers can be seen
Rising above the sea

394

Frustration poisons the soul with bitterness
Caused by running to and fro
Seeing nothing beyond the forest trees
In the wilderness of this life

The messengers came to my poverty room
Drifting upon a cloud of sorrow
They lowered their heads in the Passion of Loss
Waiting for me to know

I knew that someone dear was gone
To walk the shores of Heaven

There lived a lady named Maggie Cone
Whose name froze the marrow of every bone
In modern days of business lore
She bore a heart of winter stone…
    Maggie lived and died alone

She ruled from a soul of ice and fire
Over every prisoner in the office mire
Pearls around her neck she wore
Underneath a face of lovely ire…
    To tyranny she did aspire

Unmarried without a family
Traveling the world frantically
Her name bore whispers through every shore
Her fame grew necromantically…
    From sea to shining sea

One day she vanished without a trace
They wondered why she slowed her pace
Praying it was forevermore
Grieving to forget her gloomy face…
    Avoiding her dreary space

No one mourned for Maggie Cone
When they learned her life had flown
Not a single tear they bore
For the lady with the heart of stone…
    Maggie lived and died alone

78th Assembly

397

Pain is a mystery

Friend

Enemy

Deliverance—

Salvation

398

Here along the Ivory Shore
Where fair-skinned beauty is queen
There are women of Nubian Blood
Whose beauty is as the night

Their eyes are like the stars of Heaven
Their smile is as the moonlight
They are lovely as the Dark'ned Sea
Underneath a moonlit night

Three women

Who were little girls in 1864

Lived alone in a house of dread

Where spirits roamed the floor

Spirits of the Dead...

Three women

Who were young and free a century before

Cast spells above each other's bed

When Death came through the door

The Spirit of the Dead...

Three women

Who were old as Perpetuity and Lore

Haunted in their house of dread

When Death had won the war

Three Spirits of the Dead...

400

He watched his wife come through the door
With a message from beyond
She terrified him to the core
With the fearful expression that she bore

79th Assembly

401

When the Lady wails the moonlit night
Pray it entails beyond thy sight
Her icy touch brings Pain and Death
If thou obeyest not thine lust for flight!

Run, young bachelor!
Run!

402

It is the place where insanity lives
Where sanity goes to die
My time was spent in the Snake Room
Bound so that I could not move

Now the snake charmers have come for me
To haul me off to a lonely grave
Where I shall weep and howl for blood
Until my life has gone away

I should like to stay in the Snake Room
Where my sanity has come to die

The future is all that there is

Choices made before they are made

Paths already chosen

Rights and wrongs, consequences preborn…

Predestined

Before the earth was formed

Every life was known

Every pattern was shown

Every death

There is a world that exists beyond the twilight

A place where every future is grown

404

Intelligence screams from darkened skies
While contempt boils beneath the surface
Fear acknowledges the River of Power
From which lascivious speech emanates

Underneath gray skies
Drivers take the wrong path
Going upward when straight forward
Would have been the way

Power rolls helplessly downhill
Uncertainty bubbles into the sky
Exploding devastation all around

There are those who would seem to know the way
Who have become lost in the Poverty Field
While Death careens at the helpless soul
Cowering in fear

The gifted one makes an attempt at emergence
Assistance
Having no ability for the journey Beyond the Gate
Hearing daemons whisper old lies in a new way

Seeing the faces of youth

80th Assembly

Even while demons mock me
Laughingly
A melody of manic ingenuity
Sings in the air around me

Hauntingly

da-da-dum
    da-da-dum
        da-da-dum,

                    dum…

                            dum…

Evil comes in Crimson Red
Whirling outside my window
From night infinity's darkest dread
Arrives a demonic crescendo

SATAN stares through eyes of green
Seeking whom he may devour
Eyes in the color of Serpentine
Having Hellish ingenuity and power

Swirling storms in lustful sin
Given form from deep within
Devastation looms above the earthen shore
Whirling time and time again

Humanity walks the dark'ned maze
From the Garden of Antiquity
Speeding toward the end of days
Burning with iniquity

SATAN stares through eyes of green
Seeking whom he may devour
I saw Death in the Color of Serpentine
In humanity's final hour

Strolling University Lane
Below where lasciviousness lives and breathes
Friends drift from days before
Drowning in iniquity

Phantoms of what used to be
Revealing what is no more
Abominations threaten to corrupt the Whitened Soul
Indisputably

Winds sway
Blowing down the Trees of Life
Swirling across the Campus of Dreams
Hope waits for insanity's plea

Evil floods the river valley
Beneath the forest grove of trees
Trees of sinister intention
Too fearful for comprehension

As the tempest whirls above the house
I gaze outside my window
The living trees blew a wicked cry…
Hoping for me to die

From deep within the forest grove
One tree moved near to where I lay
Showing me its wicked face
While I trembled in my hiding place

The tree twisted up from the flooded ground
Crashing itself upon the house
To kill underneath a stormy sky…
Waiting for me to die

81st Assembly

409

When she realizes you should never have taken it

That first step will be the death of you…

So don't take it

410

Walking through the Grieving Land
I see the towering Trees of Life
While angels of darkness are behind me
Whispering incongruities

Trees of great beauty and power
Rising high above the Land of Poverty
Three trees lost in winter's sleep
With promises to blossom

Somewhere in this hour of bereaving
Lives every ghost of past sorrow
Haunting the Palace of No Prosperity
Enticing me unto death

411

Inside my House of Isolation
Underneath the pouring rain
Lies emanate from my working station
Filling my grieving heart with pain

412

The hopeless wanders to and fro
Seeking a place to call her own
Having no knowledge of where to go
Braving the wilderness time alone

In regret for seven times seventy seven
Waiting for her pain to cease
In mourning for the Shores of Heaven
Grieving for a day of peace

In the light of a rising Harvest Moon
Weeping for a place to roam
Her soul sings a melody in tune
When the Angel comes to call her Home

82nd Assembly

413

As Christ our Lord was born in a stable
Greatness is born from obscurity
Thereafter is a time so filled with heartache
That there is no desire to remember it

The Road to Greatness is terrible indeed
Racked with the pain and sorrow of Hell
Agony and Fear are upon this road…
This path

414

Weep not for the dead
They are beyond human concern
Receiving their just reward
For the life they lived

415

If it's not broken
Then why try to fix it?
Greatness has its own purpose
Its own way of being

While quartets play harmonies of false hope
Longing for what might have been
Portraits of the Great Composer appear
As a sign from perpetuity…

The straws of a broom cannot be separated
Then reattached by hand
One cannot tamper with what is Perfection
To do so is a grievous error

416

A young boy drifted to my room
In the woes of pain and frustration
His arms were as skinny as skeleton bones
His body bore the strain of starvation

"You must remember to eat" I said,
"No wonder your body is thin"
He touched his hand to his tiny throat
Where he had felt his sickness begin

For two weeks the boy suffered through this pain
Time and time again
It became not a question of *if* he would die
But rather a question of *when*

83rd Assembly

417

If BEETHOVEN is the God of Melody
And MOZART is his King
Who alone is the Crown Prince
Of Melodies to sing?

Italy is his homeland
Bel Canto wears his ring
ROSSINI is the clowning Crown Prince
Of Melodies to sing!

In the heart of memory
The grass harp plays a melody in tune
To whisper dreams of those who have gone
And of those who were once forgotten

From the Shores of Eden to Gethsemane
To the Garden of Eternity

Phantoms drift from times before
To breathe solace upon a troubled soul
Wishing joy and happiness for days to come
Soothing regret for days that have gone away

Heaven rains comfort for souls in grieving
So they will know that life must travel on
From the Shores of Eden to Gethsemene
To the Garden of Eternity

Souls lift upon winds of mercy
Carried to the Golden Gates of Heaven
While the Spirit eases those who are left behind
Until their blessed day is come

Wickedness abounds…

In today's Heart of Luxury
Children are being corrupted
By their parents' crooked souls

He was wounded for our transgressions
He was bruised for our iniquities

Phantoms of the past and future
Threaten to eat them alive
Devouring them with sins
Until they are eaten away

Now the sign of the Cross
Is spread across the entire earth
A message of Love in crimson
A sacrifice born in blood

He was wounded for our transgressions
He was bruised for our iniquities…
Then He was nailed to the accursed tree
So that we would not have to die

Elizabethan III

These are the last days
When the Spirit is poured out upon all flesh
When young men shall see visions
And old men shall dream dreams

The days when wickedness shall abound
To corrupt the Heart of Youth
To darken the souls of innocence…
To bathe the world in blood

84th Assembly

420

I rode toward the Shores of Divinity
Atop the train that was stretched to infinity

To what did before my eyes appear
The substance of what I endeavored to fear
A length of train cars had fallen away
To the depth of my intrepid soul's dismay

Now, the evening train was born in two
To shock me with what it was apt to do
Its front line slowed to a creeping crawl
Until it barely moved at all

From the mists of a lonely wilderness plain
A man and a little boy approached the train
Two souls adrift in the evening tide
Opened a train car and hid inside

Terror held me once again
As disaster approached where they were hiding in
The back line rolled to a screaming pace
Crashing into their hiding place

Elizabethan III

Their box car splintered and vanished away
Killing them in the cool of the evening day
I saw their life's blood begin to flow
Dripping down to the ground below

421

The lack of self esteem has grown
Planted in a mother's womb
Ugliness has been confirmed
Blossoming with fruit

Killers lurk in the shadows of civility
Craving to do their souls' bidding
While beauty crushes a poor soul to naught
To assure him of his calling

Those who know seek to escape from danger
Before the demons come knocking at the door
Fulfilling the promise of a painful life
Where no happiness is grown

Jade conquers the Midland Valley
After the howling brings the sail
The messengers bring evil in forked tongues
To spit venom in the eyes of the accursed

Elizabethan III

Now, the doomed walks among the simple
Seeking to escape from harm
Knowing that the demons are on his trail
Awaiting his return

Self esteem is choked at the root
Killed by the poison from her mouth

422

Hiding behind the looking glass
The wall of black awaits the happening
Lines appear through the dividing wall
Where sin can look to the other side

Lasciviousness reaches outward
Through where the looking glass is raised
A hand splits the dividing wall in two
Into the hiding place

423

Walking through the Land of the Dead
In grief upon the road to nowhere
Chariots filled with demons arrive
To offer me a ride

424

A daughter speeds away in a rocket ship
A gift given to her reluctantly
A present having come long overdue
Born from modern technology

Happiness carries the new ship aloft
High above the Land of Plenty
Soaring away from the Grieving Land
For all eternity

85th Assembly

425

From behind the Walls of Luxury
Prayers rain in abundance
Covering the landscape with ingenuity
And mountainous prosperity

426

Deception roams the world in RED
Seeking whom it may devour
There are no exceptions to be said
Evil reigns in force and power

Avoid publication on your own
Like a swim in the shark infested sea
If not you will be eaten to the bone
With no reward for your vanity

427

Somewhere in the Land of Grieving
Where the evening glows in amber light
A soul endeavors to catch a ride
To escape the coming gloom of night

428

What is the grieving land?
A place of neverending gray
There can be no wish to go there
Nor any desire to stay

Trouble runs along the death road
The road in this world of silhouette
Problems running to and fro
To proclaim thy soul's regret

429

Melancholy lives in morning fog
Rolling upon currents of gray
Reaching out to those who live
Bringing sadness to the Autumn Day

Faces look deep into eyes of pain
Drifting in the mist of gray
Speaking whispers from the Mouth of God
Blessings and Curses to fade away

86th Assembly

430

Go ahead, free yourself
There's nothing I can do
Fix yourself a travel box
And wave to my desire

Images conspire
To haunt the dream of the dead
A taste of riches that will never be
Success beyond the enlightened shore

Now, ghosts have risen
Dividing right from wrong
Teaching corruption to the harbored soul
Encouraging them to die

Right is might through spite
With delight over how contrite you can be
Wrong belongs in Kong's stronghold of a gong
Crashing it ashore

The larger aspect is guilt and human labour
Even though neither can save the soul…

From Hell

432

Technology—

Someday it will go too far

Heads on bodies they were not born upon

Unnatural life spans

A living death

433

Hope brightens a dreary day
Descending like a dove
Sending happiness the Autumn Way
With blessings from above

434

Imagine a tree of royal birth
High above the distant shore
A tree of insurmountable girth
Wisdom grown from days of lore

To see it is a dreadful thing
A sign born of infinity
Towering above the Earthen King
A prophecy from divinity

435

I climbed atop the tallest tree
To gaze as far as I could see
The sky was the glory of Ocean Blue
While green colored all the land before me

87th Assembly

436

Craving each other broken and weeping
Masquerading smiles of good will
Hearts of gossip and judgmentalism
Crumbling underneath desire

437

Genius interred at Interlaken
Of memorable ability
Golden yarns weaved in the evening day
Underneath the twilight of civility

Inspiration born in the 5th dimension
Beyond that which is known to man

He is the cruelest thing in creation
Guilt laid upon him by time
Absolved by contrition
Swirling in the Garden Way

Beyond the gates of reason
Seasons come and go intrepidly
As though no more melancholy was done
As if no more reason was left to be won

This is the season to kill
The season to die

These are days of innocence
Days lost in the calender flow
Grieving for a time of penitence
Seeking for a new place to go

Wishing for the days of spring
For a new afterlife to know
Thundering hooves from the forest ring
Gallops a white stallion in the snow

Huffing a warning to those in approach
Looking for a ride
Never burdened by the riding coach
Having no need for a place to hide

Given form by Dreams of Sneddon
Having nowhere left to go
In the aftermath of Armageddon
Running through the prairie snow

88th Assembly

440

Green girl, green girl
Where have you been?
I went around the world
And back again

Green girl, green girl
What did you see?
I saw the devil
looking at me

Green girl, green girl
What did you do?
I ran away
And came back to you

441

Stumbling in the pouring rain
Bound in drunkenness and vice
A woman dressed in blue and white
Screaming obscenities

442

Speeding towards the city lights
Underneath a cold and starlit night
We saw Death along the winding road
Roll to us with eerie spite

We died along the winding road
Underneath a cold and starry night

443

Nine banded ferocity
Attacking with velocity
Killing the life I have tried to build
With fervent reciprocity

89th Assembly

444

Shall we leave behind unloving arms—
To return to our mother's loving arms?

Mother—
Where did you come from?
Into what world did you go?

445

They built their future on a rockland tower
High above the desert sand
I heard the call of their final hour
Rumble across the Grieving Land

Crumbling sent their house of dreams
Tumbling to the ground below
In a burning cauldron of fervent screams
With too great a fear and pain to know

Now the grave will call their lives to fore
From lascivious times of evil strife
They are taken from the earthen shore…
Dying in the pride of life

A long time ago
In a land far away
I saw a river burdened with a curse
It was the curse of life

In the mist of darkness
I saw women of great stature and beauty
Walking bare out of the river
Shapely beyond the reasoning of the mind

These women were fully formed in nature
Underneath a dark and starlit night
In the fog of a misty plain
These beauties walk from the River of Life

Stepping onto the shore of this new world
At the edge of the atramental woods
Somewhere beyond the Land of Knee
This is the river which flows with a curse

Elizabethan III

It is the Curse of Life

I saw this woman walk unclothed
Through the mist to a village beyond the shores of reckoning
Deep into the Atramental Forest
Where the other women of the river live and breathe

With open arms they embrace the newest among them

Wrapping her in the swaddling cloth of her upright birth and living
There, in the heart of this distant land
Along the midnight shore

I gaze upon the figure of feminine beauty
Walking alone

Here, in the village of her dreams
She is embraced by the women of the river
Who flood her soul in kisses
To welcome her from her blessing of eternal sleep

Into the curse of life

447

Across the landscape of reason
Flows a poison
Destroying the soul of life
Where it rests…

In pain and weeping

In the halls of learning
The Angel of the Lord beheld the young man
Admiringly…
As though this young man—
Were something to see

449

As I lay still in my grieving bed
Yellow sickness pills scattered all about
The woman from the north came to me and said
"You have no further cause for doubt—

Your prophecy is come overdue
A calling from beyond the sea
Now there is business for us to do
A promise upon the Golden Key!"

450

Her ancestors stood tall and grim
In a painting on the wall
She sat still in a wooden chair
IN the painting

She sat still in a wooden chair
NEAR the painting

ABOUT THE AUTHOR

Jonathan Lovejoy is a graduate of the University of North Carolina at Greensboro, with a B.A. in Religious Studies. He currently lives in Winston Salem, North Carolina.

For more info on the author's life and career, visit jonathanlovejoy.com.

www.ingramcontent.com/pod-product-compliance
Lightning Source LLC
Chambersburg PA
CBHW060920040426
42445CB00011B/717
* 9 7 8 0 6 9 2 3 1 9 1 8 5 *